Beautiful in Black and White

January to July 2016
Photographic Memories

Author Photographer
Publisher

Ian McKenzie

ISBN-13: 978-1539356998
ISBN-10: 153935699X

BISAC: Photography /
Collections, Catalogues,
Exhibitions / General

Copyright 2016 Ian McKenzie

www.IansBooks.com

Powerhouse Park New Farm

page 1

The Powerhouse on the banks of the Brisbane River at New Farm began life as power station. It has been converted into a trendy theatre with both indoor and outdoor dining areas. On one side of the theatre is Brisbane's well known New Farm Park. On the other side is the Powerhouse Park.

The big old poinciana tree (delonix regia), is a favourite tree to climb, and it's not just for kids.

Brisbane is sometimes referred to as The River City

The Brisbane River is seen in the background behind these three photos

page 3

Fitness equipment in the park

page 4

Dancing in the park

page 5

A great place to exercise or just relax

page 6

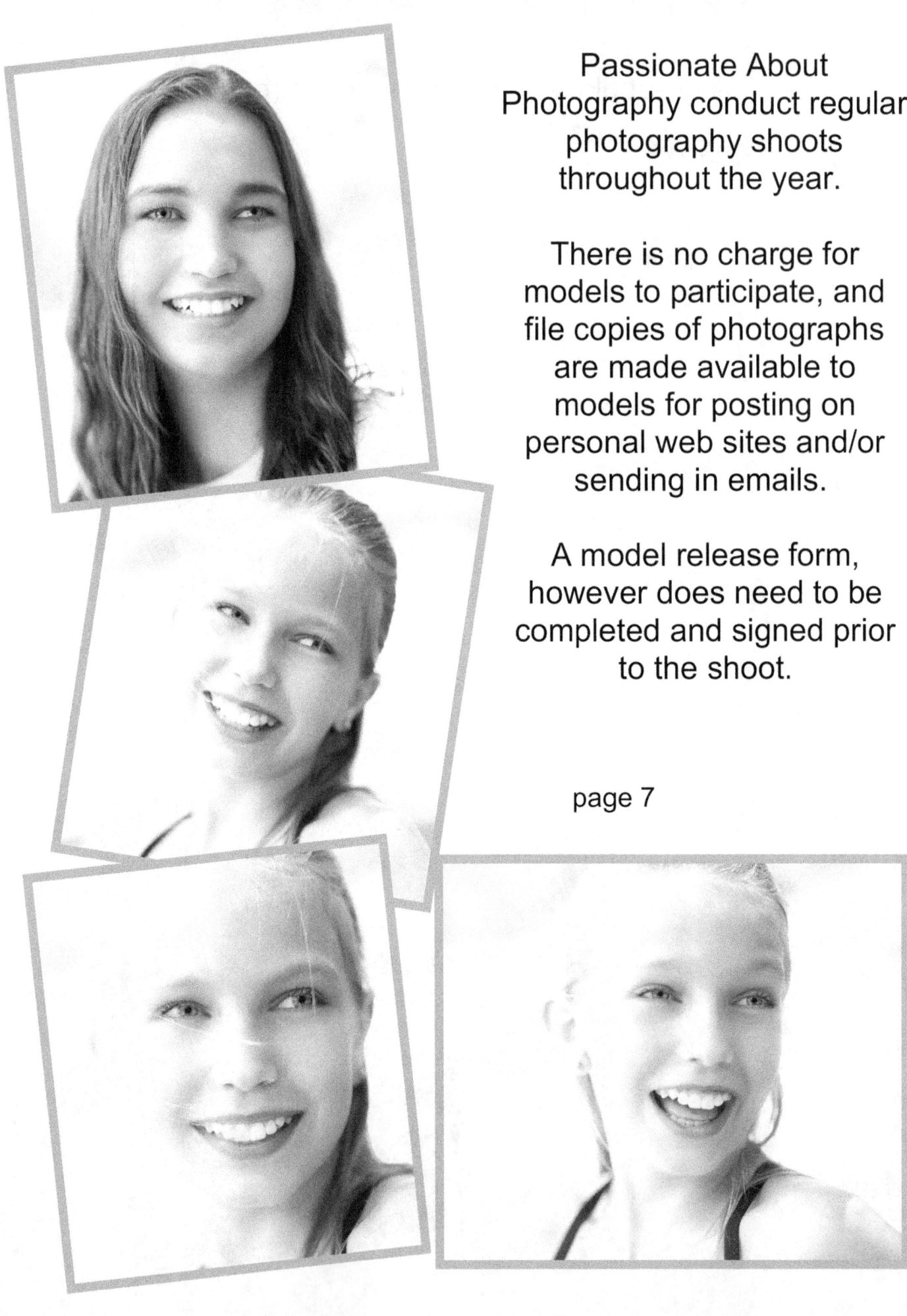

Passionate About Photography conduct regular photography shoots throughout the year.

There is no charge for models to participate, and file copies of photographs are made available to models for posting on personal web sites and/or sending in emails.

A model release form, however does need to be completed and signed prior to the shoot.

page 10

page 11

The photos on this page and the next few pages were taken at Springfield

Springfield is one of the newer suburbs on the outskirts of Ipswich city. It's close to both Brisbane city and Logan city. In recent years all these cities have merged together into one large metropolis.

page 13

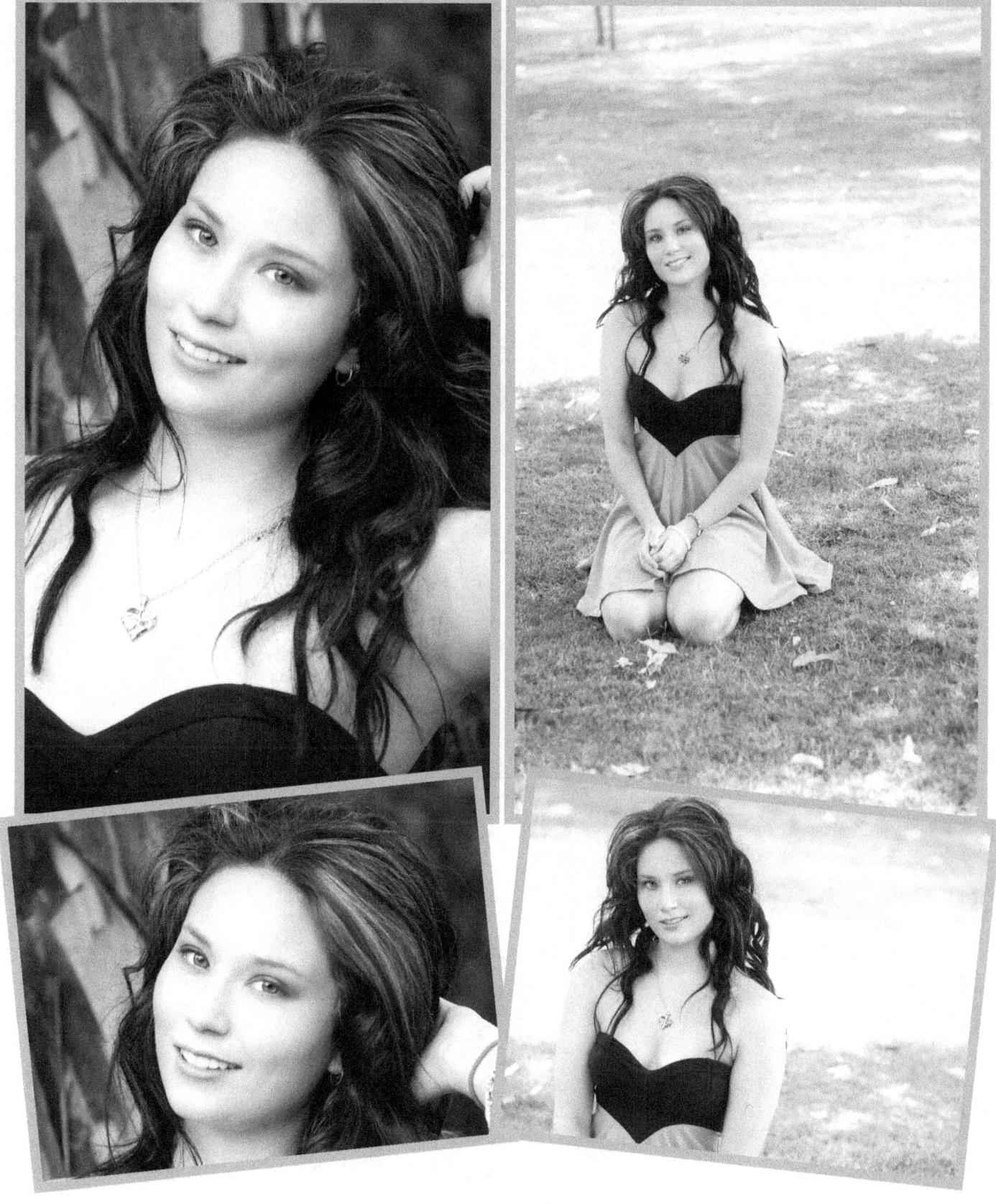

page 15

If you live in or near Brisbane and have an interest in being involved in Passionate About Photography shoots, you can obtain further information from the following web site and Facebook page:

www.passionateaboutphotography.net
www.Facebook.com/passionateaphotography

page 17

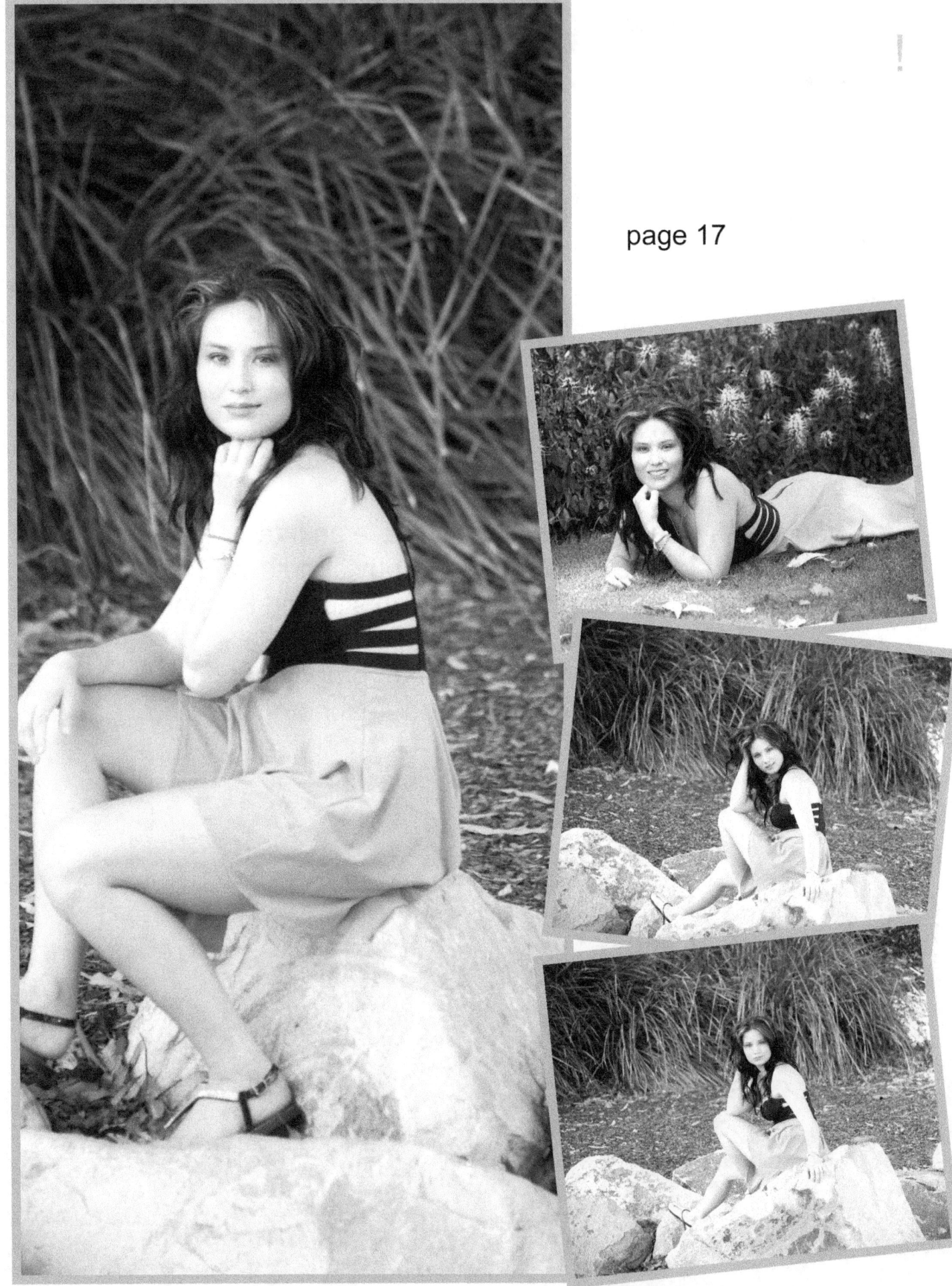

page 19

Australia Day - 26 January, 2016

page 20

page 22

page 24

page 25

page 26

page 27

The photographs on this page, the preceding pages and the following pages were taken at the Sherwood Arboritum. This is a large park in Brisbane's inner western suburbs.

page 30

page 31

page 34

page 35

page 36

page 37

page 38

page 39

page 41

page 42

page 43

page 45

page 47

page 48

page 49

page 52

page 55

page 56

page 57

page 58

page 61

page 62

page 63

page 66

page 67

page 68

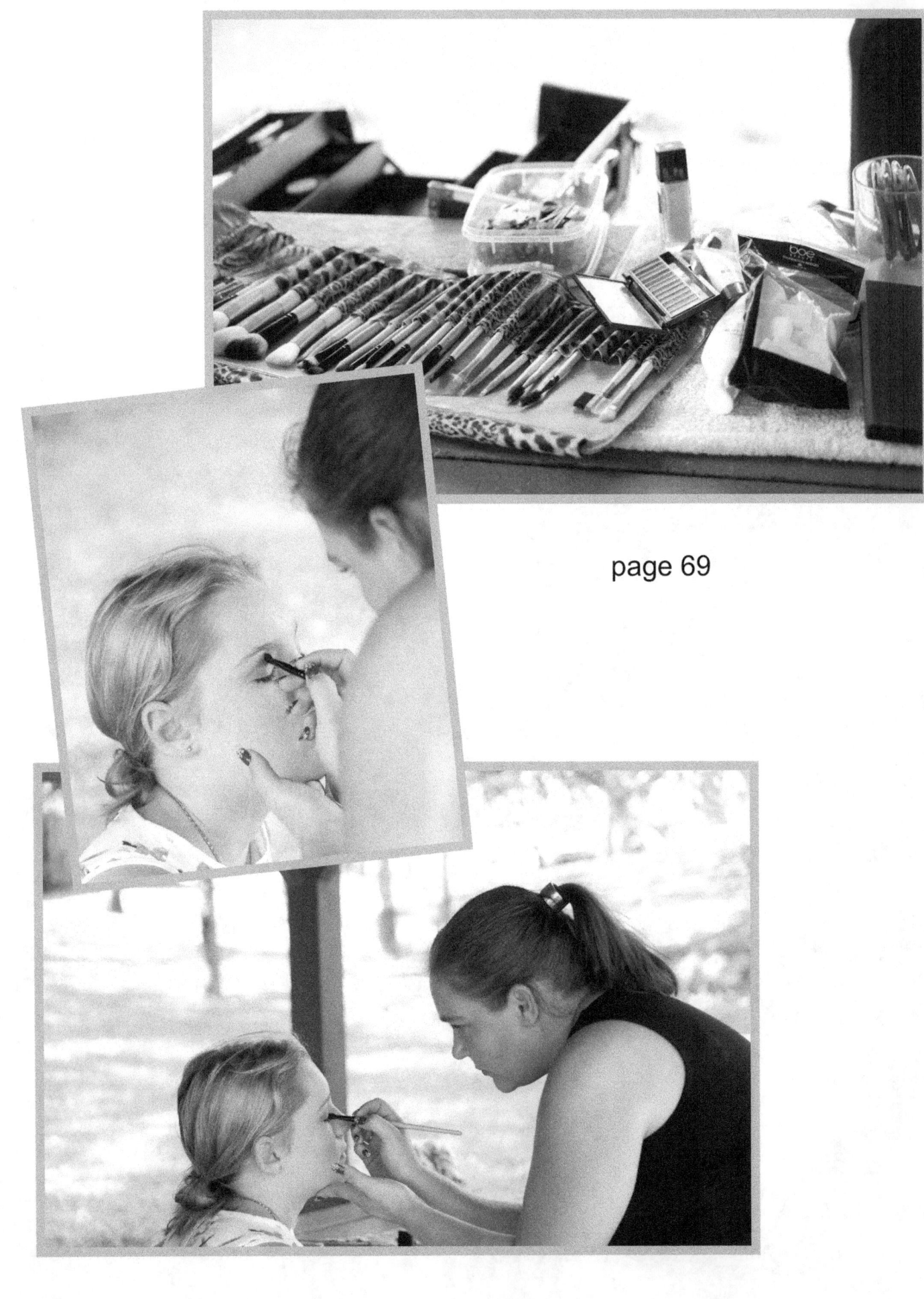

page 69

page 72

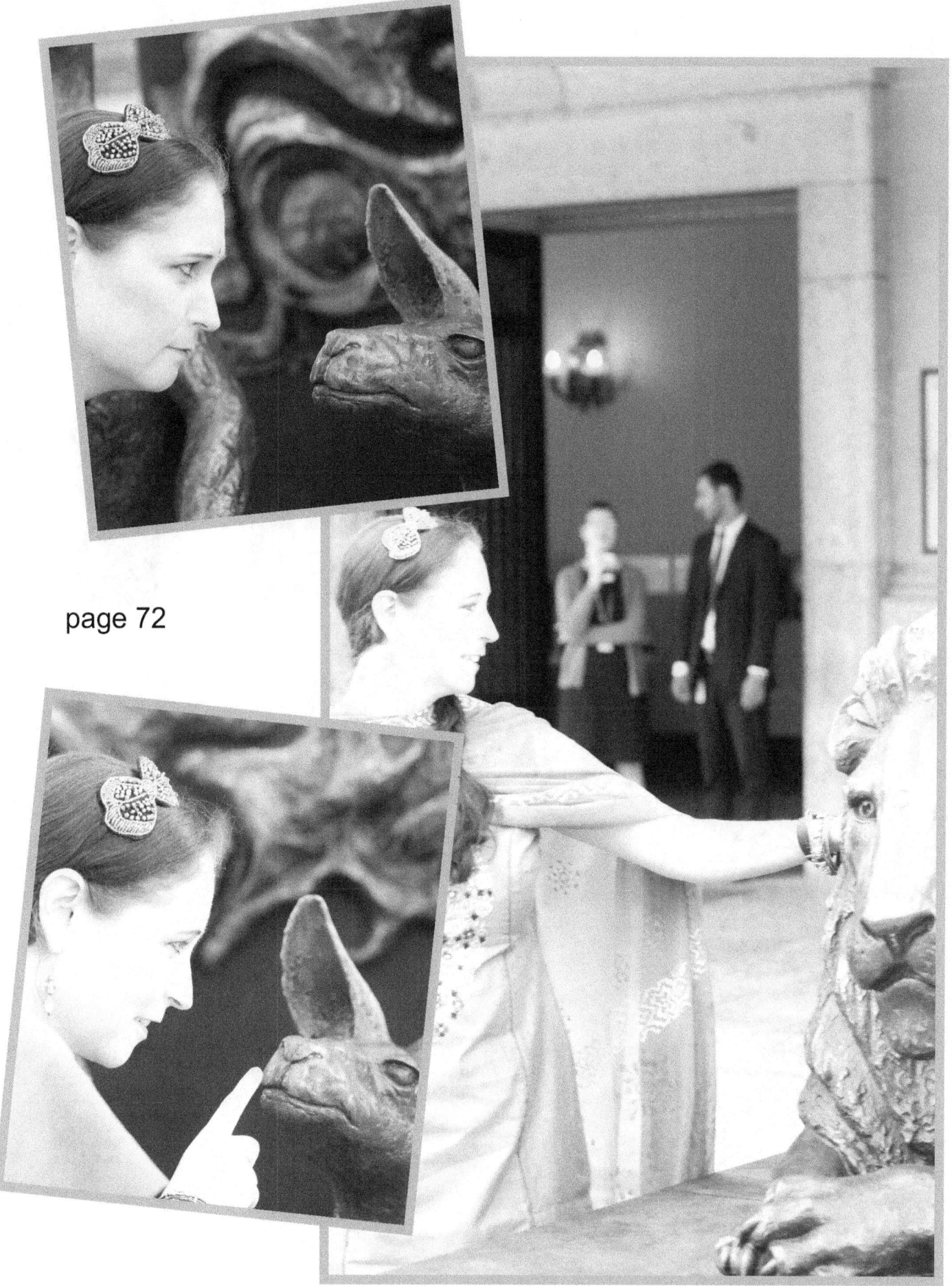

page 75

page 76

page 77

page 78

page 79

page 80

page 81

page 83

page 84

page 85

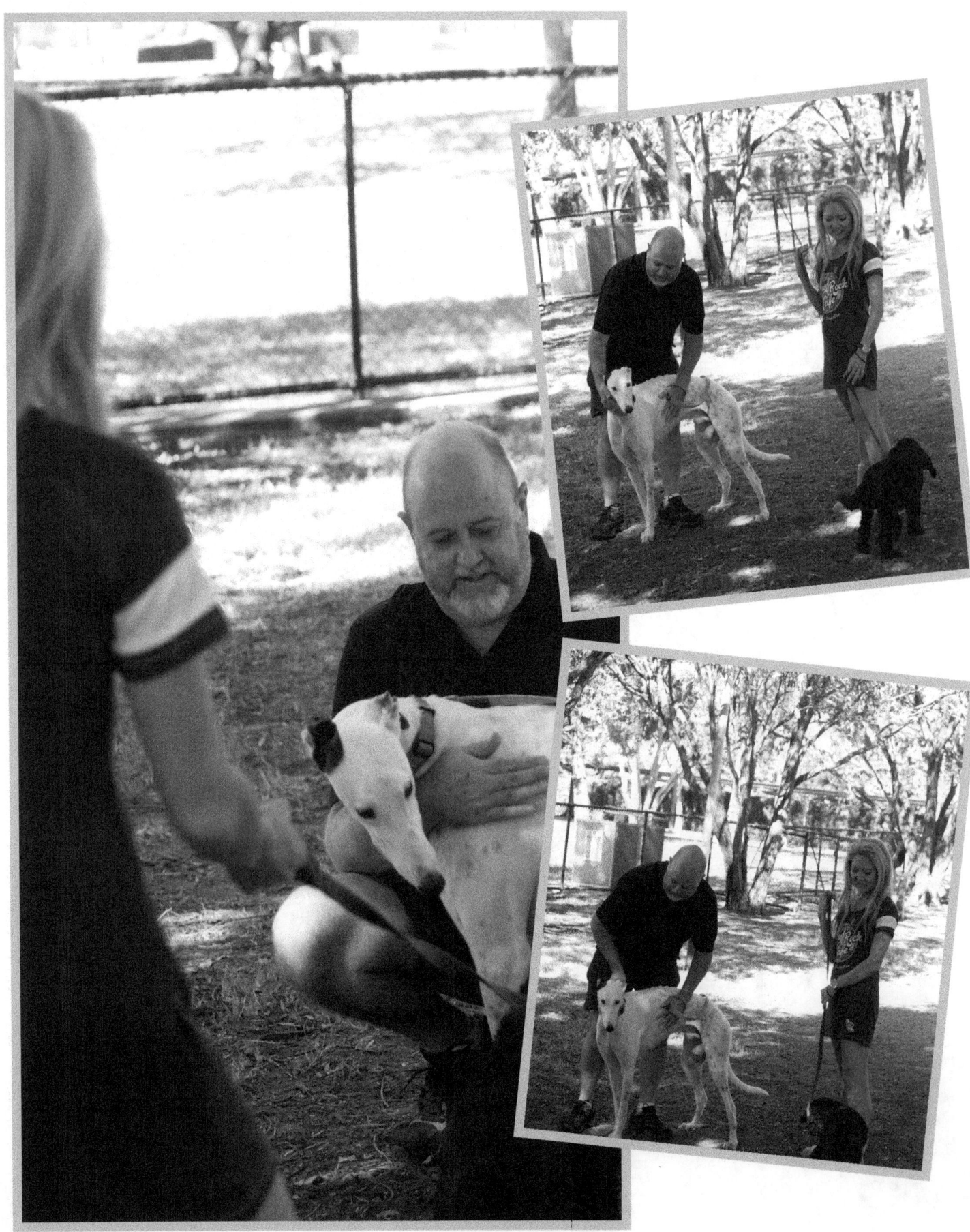

page 87

page 88

page 89

page 90

page 91

page 93

page 94

page 95

page 96

page 100

page 102

page 105

page 107

page 110

page 111

page 112

page 113

page 117